it takes love to make love.

– adrian michael

similar
titles
you
might
like.

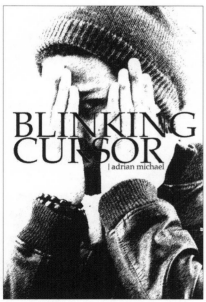

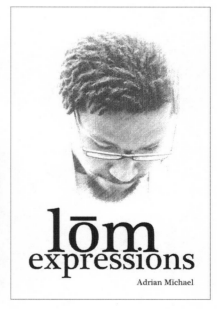

Published by A.Michael Ventures | Denver, CO
Book layout and design by GreenHigley

To contact the author visit adrianmichaelgreen.com

ISBN-13: 978-1505732627
ISBN-10: 150573262X

Printed in the United States of America

BLACK**MAGIC**

table of contents

puddles (#254)   1
love feels like (#439)   2
one drop of you (#528)   3
drink me whole (#375)   4
gasps between each breath (#255)   5
refill (#530)   6
love above sea level (#522)   7
i feel you (#418)   8
always collect her tears (#196)   9
you are a short film (#351)   10
complex (#474)   11
invisible stars (#405)   12
existential love (#401)   13
sole miner (#443)   14
you (#381)   15
she was known for making fires (#384)   16
fireworks (#400)   17
i shake when we kiss (#297)   18
i've died a thousand times (#295)   19
nothingness (#73)   19
bubbles (#299)   20
swim along your skin (#458)   21
let me become these words (#337)   22
moons eclipse (#338)   23
i see you in pixels (#415)   24
divine soul (#315)   25
i believe in magic (#389)   26
the apocalypse lives in each of us (#428)   27
become the stars (#446)   28
mantra (#447)   29
the things i'd do for you (#282)   30
the things i'd do for you ii (#201)   31

mantra ii (#413)   32
mantra iii (#414)   33
mantra iv (#436)   34
take me somewhere (#532)   35
you are enough for me (#499)   36
i can't help but hold my breath (#399)   37
our own atmosphere (#302)   38
the universe belongs to you (#308)   39
ebon skin (#286)   40
you are magic (#274)   41
you are my everything (#539)   42
blotted stains (#280)   43
i have studied your lips (#277)   44
honey (#324)   45
a love supreme (#359)   46
skin (#457)   47
the demons in you (#438)   48
old soul (#437)   49
in everything you sank (#226)   50
the best kind of humans (#513)   51
heat stroke (#406)   52
mosaic (#289)   53
tango (#314)   54
the equation (#423)   55
human (#540)   56
even lovers must rise from the ashes (#534)   57
not of this place (#366)   58
wild thing (#368)   59
tenderness (#310)   60
i feel i could burst (#312)   61
when you least expect it (#234)   62
love language (#336)   63
infatuation (#329)   64
she isn't broken (#328)   65

the perfect sunrise (#236)   66
the perfect match (#250)   67
we must burn (#476)   68
common man (#507)   69
my bones would fracture first (#503)   70
you aren't of this world (#477)   71
kiss you without touch (#503)   72
sometimes i bury our love (#467)   73
magic is your skin (#362)   74
getting there is worth it (#243)   75
love magic (#225)   76
i feel you ii (#460)   77
sunflower (#357)   78
the void (#450)   79
healing energy (#524)   80
pure magic (#461)   81
burden me (#444)   82
sometimes (#492)   83
her poetry is magic (#497)   84
love is like water (#427)   85
lighthouse (#287)   86
mighty sol (#311)   87
the little things (#264)   88
one word (#266)   89
you are the universe (#419)   90
everything is going somewhere (#265)   91
love is love (#422)   92
eternity (#512)   93
loving you is my religion (#478)   94
lovers at daybreak (#486)   95
where love was first discovered (#254)   96
inside of us (#508)   97
from the earth you came (#465)   98
mantra v (#509)   99

laughter is love (#258)   100
our kind of fights (#246)   101
love whisperer (#462)   102
pain makes us human (#500)   103
love is light (#240)   104
fill me with it (#354)   105
honest lover (#374)   106
wanderlust souls (#376)   107
dark pieces (#432)   108
hate is dysfunctional love (#538)   109
taken (#526)   110
heal your wounds (#442)   111
condemned to love (#221)   112
love on some you (#510)   113
forgetting to breathe (#349)   114
every inch of me (#480)   115
homemade distillery (#475)   116
smile (#411)   117
love looks good on you (#410)   118
stardust on your bones (#459)   119
cast me into your play (#454)   120
timeless monogamy (#434)   121
magic firestorms (#516)   122
the sunrise inside of you (#531)   123
love affair (#440)   124
love is the faith my soul practices (#515)   125
breath (#523)   126
victimless crime (#448)   127
breaking point (#517)   128
trojan horse (#433)   129
tipsy (#521)   130
maybe (#506)   131
blackmagic (#170)   132
cure (#533)   133

fear (#525)   134
love is (#34)   135
alchemist (#426)   136
beautiful time bomb (#445)   137

BLACK**MAGIC**

adrian michael
BLACK**MAGIC**

<u>puddles</u>

love,
it's not a race
take it slow
we are
icicles
clenched
on fences
soon to be
puddles
on the ground

love feels like

love feels like diving deep in our souls and riding a tidal wave to shore, hand in hand, heart in heart.

love is felt deep in our bones, sheltered in marrow, replicating love-cells flooding our entire body. do you feel it? it climbs up and out and glows through our skin, radiation pierces the soul unlocking paradise within.

love feels like swallowing forevers down our throats and drinking stars to quench our thirst. ectasy is our destiny and love is our magic carpet.

my dear, love feels and tastes like sweet honey, and i never want to be without the nectar that sustains me.

i feel your soul and you fill mine.

2

adrian michael
BLACKMAGIC

one drop of you

one drop of you
isn't enough
one touch from you
isn't enough
give me tons
give me infinity
i desire as much of you
as possible

drink me whole

i would let
the ocean
drink me whole
drown my lungs
sea-salt my skin
just for a close-up
of you
my moon

gasps between each breath

let me be
the gasps
between
each breath
so i
can feel
what it's like
for you
to catch yourself
and
so you
can know
i'm always there
in moments
you never thought
possible
for anyone
to exist

adrian michael
BLACK**MAGIC**

refill

on those
long long days
that stretch my limbs
and tug at my heart
i face wild winds
i turn to the west
and let my eyes
breathe life
back into my soul
by looking out
out to where you
may have looked
to take in your energy
to refill with your air;
i need that
i need you

<u>love above sea level</u>

oh how you have reached
into the core of me
pitched a tent
made camp
survived my weather
summited my heart;
we love
above sea level
at our own elevation
you could have left
you never did

i feel you

i feel you
in the miles
that carry us
away
from each other
the odometer
in our hearts
doesn't count
distance
but records
memories
and darling,
my sweet
sunflower,
all the beats
in my body
hum
your name

adrian michael
BLACK**MAGIC**

always collect her tears

and when she cries
a star in the universe shutters
and draws me near
a cosmic barometer
gauging her weather
so no matter how far
our worlds part
i will always
collect
her
tears

you are a short film

you are a short film;
the slow-motion
dramatic
romantic
black & white classic
fleeting melodic
i-hope-we-make-it
tear jerking musical anthem
never ending story.

i just hope to be
in the ending credits
s c r o l l i n g
next to you
hand-in-hand
fading
en la distancia

complex

you can't paraphrase my love

<u>invisible stars</u>

"do you have
any tattoos?"

before she could
say anything

i answered
my own
soliloquy

"...invisible
stars...i see
them now.

that one
up north
set me
free."

adrian michael
BLACK**MAGIC**

existential love

the caption nor the graph
you are quantum breath
dust particles
suspended in air
one glimpse of you
breaks the speed
of light
and that milli
of a second
i smiled
and then
you dissappeared;
you
are
existential
love

sole miner

the tint
on my skin
contains
black
magic
diamonds
and you
are the
sole
miner

adrian michael
BLACK**MAGIC**

<u>you</u>

you took a chance on me
when no one else would

you made me face the sun
when i wanted to run

you unscrambled my wordplay
when it was meant to be ambiguous

you breathed purpose in my heart
and ever since
it has never skipped a beat

adrian michael
BLACKMAGIC

<u>she was known for making fires</u>

she was known
for making fires
with her smile
and the only one
who could
put them out

16

fireworks

i have tasted your soul
full of lavender and honey
my sol-d vision
has replaced
three-dimensional vanity
and this chest
is full of light;
it was you
it was you
that placed the sun
in my ribcage
filled my heart
with the moon & stars
you,
my dear,
are fireworks
beautiful
magic

adrian michael
BLACK**MAGIC**

i shake when we kiss

you
p a r a l y z e
my entire soul;
no words
no sound
no movement:
you
are
so
powerful,
i shake
when we
kiss

18

i've died a thousand times

if looks could kill
i've died a thousand times
and you,
you bring me
back to life

nothingness

let's say our goodbyes now so i can
experience what it's like to be without
you. get back together so the worries
about what it would feel like with you
gone dissolve into nothingness.

<u>bubbles</u>

i hold my breath
to keep from drowning;
your love
is like deep sea diving
and it is you
that reminds me
to inhale slow and steady
taking your air in
and loving you
all the way out.

i love
the bubbles
we make

adrian michael
BLACKMAGIC

<u>swim along your skin</u>

let me swim along your skin
to cruise honey waters
windsurf your sea
dive down below the surface
and find hidden treasures;
your skin
is a wonder of the world

let me become these words

let me become these words
sprawled on parchment &
spread my ashes
past the margins
because i want to lay next to
every halfway decent stanza
i've professed to you;
all that is left
will be for my alphabetic soul
to kiss yours
forever

<u>moons eclipse</u>

if you mind the gap between my
head and my heart then you must
stomach my sinkholes.

if you withstand the ebbs and flows
of my moods then, and only then,
my dear, our moons eclipse.

i see you in pixels

i see you in pixels
microscopic bits
cosmic wavelengths
others might like you
simply zoomed
all the way out
to see the perfect picture
clean & clear & crystal
not i
i prefer up close
blurred lines
jagged edges
undefined colors
to examine
the real you
below atomic-level
to lay with &
cherish
your sediment
soul

divine soul

i believe in humanity
even when my bones quake
and shutter when i hear and see
devastation;
you are a divine soul and as your
footsteps sail this dimension of time
i hunger for others to be as pure
and human as you; the kind that
has a heart big enough, words
gentle enough
to extend i love you's
as tears fall from such a sincere vessel
may there be more of you
we need you
and your pools of hope
don't give up on us
don't give up on me

<u>i believe in magic</u>

i believe
in magic
it's in
our dna

adrian michael
BLACK**MAGIC**

the apocalypse lives in each of us

the apocalypse
lives in each of us
it's just that
love
keeps our end
slowly at bay

become the stars

when our
light years
burn out
we will
fizzle
and
become
the stars

mantra

when she lets you in
protect her heart

adrian michael
BLACKMAGIC

the things i'd do for you

i would
crawl
on fractured
ground
after standing
with arms and eyes
flexed to the sky
pleading
for the sun
to always
keep you
warm;
utter madness
the things
i'd do
for you

the things i'd do for you ii

promise me one thing:
when the sun grows cold
you will not move an inch
i will move mountains
and cut through the clouds
to bring back the warmth
you give me

<u>mantra ii</u>

protect your queen

<u>mantra iii</u>

protect your king

mantra iv

love your love

take me somewhere

take me somewhere
anywhere really
i don't care much
about the destination
i care about
the journey
with you
next to you
around you
beside you
into the unknown
to a galaxy of just us

<u>you are enough for me</u>

no,
i do not wish
there were
more of you;
you
wouldn't be
you
if there were
others
camouflaged
trying to be you;
you
are
enough
for
me

i can't help but hold my breath

admiring you
i can't help
but hold my
breath;
you
are
an
underwater
beauty
that floods
my lungs

our own atmosphere

i can't compete
hell,
i'm not even
in the same
stratosphere
as the sun
moon & stars
yet
if you
let me
i'll
take you past
pluto
and you and i
will
make our own
atmosphere

<u>the universe belongs to you</u>

the universe
belongs to you
it's yours
and my one request
   a meager and selfish plea:
will you
can you
do you mind
drizzling your white lights
like spring rain showers
airbrushed across the sky;
i beg for them
hoping one of your stars
will fall
within
my reach

ebon skin

your tears
o, how they
river dance
down
down
your ebon skin.
no,
do not
wipe them away
let the waters
find their way
back
to where
they belong

<u>you are magic</u>

you are magic
the kind that
hypnotizes
the soul
& pinpoints
broken bones
& detached sinew;
you
are
the benevolent spell
that scoops
  up the pieces
making me whole
again

adrian michael
BLACKMAGIC

<u>you are my everything</u>

babe,
give me nothing
i already have enough
you are my everything
a gift i unwrap
day in and day out

blotted stains

i will share
all that i am
plastering
penned ink
not wasting
any of its
spatter.
all that i am
is the sum
of all of you
and the winds
will carry
these words
until the end
of time
and all that
remains
will be
blotted stains
of us

i have studied your lips

i have studied your lips
every line, dip and bend
and
come to realize
one truth:
the way you move
is in perfect
unison with
the perk
and pout
of your mouth
orating coded syllables
only i can make out

<u>honey</u>

my goodness
the honey on your bones
blushes through your skin

adrian michael
BLACKMAGIC

a love supreme

you are my queen
i am your king
a love supreme

46

adrian michael
BLACK**MAGIC**

skin

let me explore
each tiny scab
that bumbs your skin
i may find wounds
you had never known
existed

47

<u>the demons in you</u>

the demons in you
give sanctuary
to the demons in me
and they dance
oh how they dance

<u>old soul</u>

i'm an old soul
that believes in
chivalry, romance,
and love

<u>in you everything sank</u>

in you everything sank
and the pull of you
is equal to that of the moon;
i am a body of water
whose tides can't help
but be attracted, like magnets,
rising and falling
in your presence or absence

inspired by pablo neruda

the best kind of humans

the best kind of humans are those that stand in the fire with you. they don't abandon you when you're shattered on the rocks, they help pick up the pieces.

if you left me while broken, you aren't worth my time when i'm whole.

inspired by r.m.drake

heat stroke

being with you
is like
living close
   extremely close
to the equator;
you divide me
into two
hemispheres
and balance
my darkness
and my
light

mosaic

i would break myself
into tiny
tiny pieces
and flip them over
to show you
even when shattered
i am
but a mosaic
and you
are the artist

tango

you have consumed my soul
and tangoed with it
quick
quick
slow
i never had a chance

the equation

love is an elixir
magic + emotion

human

i am human
which means
i can be selfish
locked into myself
but
i do love you
shown in my own way
this stone wall
will come down
has come down
just for you

adrian michael
BLACK**MAGIC**

even lovers must rise from the ashes

when the world turns its back on you
and you feel all alone, when no one
will listen and you're on your own,
when the cold pavement is your only
pillow, when your heart is crushed
and you fall numb to your knees,
when you're at your lowest remember
one thing: even lovers must rise from
the ashes.

not of this place

my love
is not
of this
place

the
physics
of it
is
bound
to other
forces

wild thing

you are a wild thing
    too wild to seek approval
you are a free spirit
    too free to need validation
you are a unique soul
    too unique to be compared
you are an exquisite creature
    too exquisite to dim

tenderness
<u>tenderness</u>

"do we all deserve love?"
asked the one with many fears
"yes, we do"
responded the other
and wiped those fears away;
sometimes when we speak
all we are asking for
all that we really need
is tenderness
to mend a broken heart

adrian michael
BLACK**MAGIC**

i feel i could burst

i feel i could burst
like a butterfly
from its cocoon
spread these limbs
take flight
and jump
jump out of this skin
into yours
and e x p l o d e
becoming one;
even at an atomic level
you radiate matter
and i hope
my negative
and your positive
particles
beautifully mate

adrian michael
BLACK**MAGIC**

<u>when you least expect it</u>

in the blink
of an eye
it can happen,
faster than
you
would ever
think;
this love thing
will lay dormant,
sleep still,
and bleed out
when you least
expect it

62

love language

love is a language understood
without words

infatuation

"why this infatuation
with the stars,
the moon,
the sun?"

those...
are smoke signals
a warning
that you're near

the sky
a beacon
i gravitate &
wander
towards
all things
that
cosmically
remind me
of you

adrian michael
BLACKMAGIC

she isn't broken

she isn't broken
and her bones aren't delicate
the only fracture
is the break between her lips
and if she wills it
the space between air and sound
will let you in
and all she may need
is for you
to listen;
she has saved herself
far too many times
not everyone needs rescuing

the perfect sunrise

worry worry
the natural reaction
when your
heart skips a beat
after encountering
the perfect sunrise,
and you are sent
into outer space
with a magic kiss;
worry worry
worry no more
it is not worry at all
you're in love
you're in love

the perfect match

panic is the souls way
of finding equilibrium
when it comes into contact
with the perfect match—
love can feel like a heart attack
just breathe it all in

adrian michael
BLACK**MAGIC**

we must burn

we must burn
to ignite
our aptitude
to love
fully
to live
passionately

common man

i
am a common man
with an ordinary love
for wild souls

adrian michael
BLACK**MAGIC**

my bones would fracture first

trust
that i will
catch you
if you fall
my bones
would fracture first
before harm
comes to you

you aren't of this world

you aren't of this world
you've destroyed
the homogeneity
of my existence
selfishly i wish
my presence
blemished
some or all
of your
heart's horizon

kiss you without touch

loving you is all i can give and i promise
to always provide a complete love. even
if my all falls short, know the intention is
to kiss you without touch.

adrian michael
BLACK**MAGIC**

sometimes i bury our love

sometimes i bury our love
under bedrock and wait for it
to crack sediment
testing my hypothesis
that what we have is powerful and real

adrian michael
BLACKMAGIC

magic is your skin

magic is your skin
the way it talks with the sun

getting there is worth it

love is a mountain
with no way around;
up and thru
is the only option.
when you reach the summit
and stake your claim
the bumps and bruises
headaches and anguish
will be replaced with
sighs of relief
and tears of disbelief
in awe of part one
of a journey's end;
getting there is worth it:
love,
your new oxygen has been waiting
but
you'll never know
what you've been missing
until you get there
so start the climb
you must

love magic

like a spark plug
you ignite my soul
sending super-sonic
waves of electricity
hardwiring every little detail
energizing each heartbeat
causing uncontrollable
smirks and smiles;
you must have love magic
that fires up air and gas
shooting silent
but heavenly sparks
that dance on the epidermis
and melt

a d r i a n m i c h a e l
BLACK**MAGIC**

i feel you ii

you are entitled
to your feelings
and every experience
in between
i may not feel them
but i feel you
and that's
plenty enough
for me

sunflower

"why are you so warm?"
i asked with sleep
in my eyes.

"because i'm a sunflower:
full of sun," she said
wide awake.

<u>the void</u>

i often sit aside
in dark corners of my mind
and drift
i escape my forest thoughts
and stare
as far into the void as i can
pitch black silence
pitch black om vibrations
and there you are
etched in my shadows
keeping me safe;
i couldn't imagine
what this place
would be like
if you
were
absent

<u>healing energy</u>

you know my demons
by name
and call them out
to free me
from myself;
you
are
healing
energy

pure magic

i believe
in magic;
not knowing
how you
just appeared
out of thin air
and
rescued
my soul...
it wasn't
a trick
it was
pure
magic

adrian michael
BLACK**MAGIC**

burden me

let me hold
all of the weight
you have carried
not because
it's too heavy
nor am i stronger
but because
you deserve
to rest;
burden me
for it is no burden
at all

<u>sometimes</u>

sometimes
flowers
don't
want you
to be
gentle

her poetry is magic

her poetry is magic
the kind that's
not fad or fashion

she is soul
she is mystic
she
is
outstanding &
uncommon;
a celestial
human being
she is.

love is like water

love is like water:
powerful enough to drown you
soft enough to cleanse you
deep enough to save you

lighthouse

you
are
an everlasting
flame
flickering
staying lit
through
any weather;
a lighthouse
in
all
chaos
i seek
your glow
heat &
smoke;
don't
   i beg of you
put out the light
don't put out the light

mighty sol

the sun shines
when she's away
it's like
the further she travels
the sun comes closer
as if
a memorandum
of understanding exists
to keep me warm
so she won't be missed;
she
is a mighty sol

the little things

staring out this window
watching snow fall
wing-tipped ice spatters
on glass
    it dances
    it glides
    with such grace
the bounce of sound
harmonizes the descent
as my sight becomes
cascaded with white
and my body temp declines
you surround me
with innocent frozen raindrops
showcasing just one
of many ways
how you are always around
in the little things

adrian michael
BLACK**MAGIC**

one word

if i had one word
left to say
let me live in silence
until that fateful day
when all that i have
built up and mustered
vibrates from my vocal chords
and escapes passed my lips
after i've seen
and seen again and again
the lift of your walk
the twist of your hips
the sway of your shoulders
the curl of your hair
the movement of your mouth
then and only then
will i let my final word rest

<u>you are the universe</u>

you
are
the
universe,
every
crescent
moon

everything is going somewhere

everything
is going somewhere
and the magic
in your eyes
is but the roadmap
amongst the stars
leading me
leading you
to that somewhere
somehow
someway

adrian michael
BLACK**MAGIC**

<u>love is love</u>

there is them
there is us
they may have
what we want
we may have
what they want
either way
we are us
they are them
love is love
luv es lov
we are them
they are us

<u>eternity</u>

love,
don't give your energy
to just anyone;
give it to me
and i will love only you
for all eternity

adrian michael
BLACKMAGIC

<u>loving you is my religion</u>

the idea of you
was beautiful

meeting you
was spiritual

loving you
is my religion

94

lovers at daybreak

you are.
i am.
we are.
stars in the distance.
lovers at daybreak.

where love was first discovered

i've sailed
above the clouds
even visited
the ninth one
and realized
that
you've taken
me further
to places
much higher
than where
clouds
are formed.

       you,
       my lover,
       are the
       spaceship
       that blasts us off
       beyond
       the planetary system
       where love
       was first discovered

adrian michael
BLACK**MAGIC**

inside of us

our hearts
beat poetry
that don't rhyme
that don't blend
that don't make sense.
our hearts
beat poetry
that challenge
that temper
that instigate
bohemian sonnets
written on our
tongues
and moved
by the pounding
volcano
waiting
to erupt
inside of us

from the earth you came

from the earth you came
and the core of you
fires my whole entire
body;
my soul
my soul
you shook
you shook

mantra v

when he lets you in
protect his heart

<u>laughter is love</u>

laughter is love
busting at the seams
coming up for air

our kind of fights

our kind of fights
shake the earth
and echoes into the galaxy
returning a
boomerang reminder
that
love is a struggle
worth fighting for

love whisperer

be
the
love
whisperer
but
speak
loud
with
actions
and
heal
fractured
souls

pain makes us human

pain makes us human &
pain selfishly fuels our
intense desire to love
what makes us suffer

<u>love is light</u>

love is light
creeping at windows daybreak;
release the shade
illuminate your life
and watch the sun rise.
it's the radiance alone that's...
strong enough
worthy enough
curious enough
to give a chance

fill me with it

you aren't perfect
neither am i
sun in your lungs
warm my soul
release that light
harvested within
let me feel it
fill me with it

honest lover

long-suffering
without complaint
is an honest lover
who patiently waits

<u>wanderlust souls</u>

the way your body moves
is a beautiful language
that is remnant of
african drums
beating in the distance
welcoming wanderlust souls
home

dark pieces

judge not
and hold
all
of my dark
pieces
as you would
hold
my light

<u>hate is dysfunctional love</u>

hate is dysfunctional love
trapped in obscure darkness
begging
to feel the light

<u>taken</u>

you took
my heart
my mind
my soul

heal your wounds

heal your wounds
before you jump
into someone else's

condemned to love

these trail of words will lead us
back to each instance, back to each
happenstance, back to each eye glance,
back to each beautiful fatal moment—
when our nostalgic souls dance to the
rhythm of a lifetime of happiness and
recall the how, when, what, and why's of
being condemned to love each other; a
ravishing breadcrumb tale.

<u>love on some you</u>

if you rely on the love of someone else
to lead a meaningful life, then you will
forever be at their mercy.

love on some you.

forgetting to breathe

"do you think of me all the time?"
she asked with a peak of sadness.

"i see you in everything:
even the slightest tilt of the clouds
remind me of how graceful you are, like
there is air beneath your feet and you
break the laws of gravity."

"is that so..?" a hint of sun clamored
from her mouth.

"when i don't think of you it's like
forgetting to breathe."

<u>every inch of me</u>

you loved my soul
dusted off
cobwebs &
shined my heart;
the love you give
the love you share
the love you sing
lifts &
caresses
my complex dimensions;
your loving humanity
recharges
every inch of me

homemade distillery

you are my homemade distillery;
there is a sweet science about you
that brings out all that is good
within me

adrian michael
BLACK**MAGIC**

<u>smile</u>

you make my soul smile

love looks good on you

love looks good on you
it beams
like
gatsby's
emerald green
lighthouse
at daisy's dock
in the bay:
it's so damn
intoxicating

adrian michael
BLACK**MAGIC**

stardust on your bones

verbally i am shy
but allow my written word
lay to rest
any doubt
or obtuse miscalculation
of my undying
infatuation & love
for the outline of your soul
and the stardust
on your bones

adrian michael
BLACK**MAGIC**

<u>cast me into your play</u>

cast me into your play
script out my words
block my every move
costume my character
dictate my mood
wardrobe my scenes
insert your tones
write my lyrics
direct my body language
i'll be your actor
just say action

timeless monogamy

six
infinities of
kisses
and a
lifetime
of
showing you
how much
&
how deep
i
love
you
is
timeless
monogamy

adrian michael
BLACKMAGIC

magic firestorms

you
are
magic
firestorms
that
set
aflame
my
gentle
spirit

the sunrise inside of you

of all the poets
you are my favorite
for there is nothing
nothing nothing nothing
more alluring
or breathtaking
than the sunrise
inside of you

<u>love affair</u>

be spontaneous,
be thoughtful
be in love—
keep
your appreciation
of the mind,
body and soul
at the
forefront
of your
love
affair

adrian michael
BLACK**MAGIC**

<u>love is the faith my soul practices</u>

love
is the faith
my soul
practices
on a
daily
basis

adrian michael
BLACKMAGIC

breath

love is
the long
inhale
the windy
exhale

126

<u>victimless crime</u>

love
is a
victimless
crime:
the punishment
is worth
the risk

breaking point

even lovers have a breaking point

trojan horse

you
were
the
trojan
horse
that
broke
into
my
ribcage
and
stole
my
heart

adrian michael
BLACK**MAGIC**

tipsy

tipsy
is how you
make me feel
whenever you
walk into a room

maybe

maybe
it's the harp
in your voice
and the ocean
in your tone
that makes
hearing
"i love you more"
so special
so real

blackmagic

magic isn't abra kadabra
not even alakazam
it's the passing of moments
that fuzzy little feeling
creviced when eyes meet
it's the convergence of color
pitch black hue
that tingle touch
shooting pulsed goosebumps
dancing on skin
magic is the melody in a whisper
a smile
a wink
it happens before our eyes
hidden in the simplest of things

love is
blackmagic
love is
me + you

cure

love can be a cure
if we just let it in

fear

i fear
that love
will always be
misunderstood

love is

love is.
let it be.
like wine
let it breathe.

adrian michael
BLACK**MAGIC**

<u>alchemist</u>

the alchemy
of you
turns
everything
to gold

beautiful time bomb

we may talk
as if love
wasn't messy
but in its fullness
it is chaotic
and has sharp edges
pricking and prodding
our insides
to remind us
it can be taken away
if forgotten;
love is
a beautiful
time bomb

the magic in me
honors the magic in you

BLACKMAGIC

adrian michael

ig: @adrianmichaelgreen
tw: @adrianmichaelgr
fb: /adrianmichaelgr
e: adrianmichaelgreen@gmail.com
w: adrianmichaelgreen.com

Made in the USA
Middletown, DE
07 December 2017